SHEEP DON'T GO TO SCHOOL

This book is dedicated
to my mother Vera Fusek.

With thanks to Michael Bird
who set me on the path.

Sheep Don't Go to School

edited by

ANDREW FUSEK PETERS

illustrated by

MARKÉTA PRACHATICKÁ

BLOODAXE BOOKS

ISBN: 1 85224 408 9

First published 1999 by
Bloodaxe Books Ltd,
P.O. Box 1SN,
Newcastle upon Tyne NE99 1SN.

Bloodaxe Books Ltd acknowledges
the financial assistance of Northern Arts.

Thanks are due to the Arts Council of England
for providing a translation grant for this book.

Cover printing by J. Thomson Colour Printers Ltd, Glasgow.

Printed in Great Britain by
Cromwell Press Ltd, Trowbridge, Wiltshire.

CONTENTS

INDEX OF TRANSLATORS

INTRODUCTION

Sheep Don't Go to School began after I developed an interest in my own Czech culture and translated some of the nursery rhymes my mother grew up with. The wordplay and images were delightful. In my work as a poet in education, the poems went down very well with audiences of all ages. I wondered if other countries from the former Eastern Europe had similar material. My research revealed that very little had appeared in translation in children's anthologies, apart from the work of a few well-known authors such as Miroslav Holub. After contacting poets, translators, writers and embassies all over Europe, a wealth of verse began to flood in.

The words reminded me of Edward Lear and Spike Milligan, but with a culturally recognisable style. The metaphors were very sophisticated, and the poems dealt with both the surreal and the serious. There was no talking down to children here.

One of the pieces that moved me greatly was the long Albanian poem 'The Song of Doruntina', which is a classic poem well-known to children growing up in Albania. The poem is about a mother who has lost all her sons in the war. It is quite a ghostly and sad piece. But when the translator, Elona Velca, sent it to me, it came with a note saying she had to rush back home. In the news the following week came the collapse of Albania, and the possibility of civil war. A poem that had been written hundreds of years ago suddenly seemed disturbingly relevant.

In other poems, carrots dance, walnuts wear coats, and the North Pole has opened a sweetshop for seals! There are riddles and tongue-twisters, traditional rhymes and poems from famous and classical children's authors. Material has been collected from Albania, Bielarussia, Bulgaria, the Czech Republic, Estonia, Germany, Hungary, Latvia, Lithuania, Poland, Romania, Russia and the former Yugoslavia. The many translators and poets who contributed to this book have worked hard to make their translations sparkle as brightly and rhythmically in English as in their native tongue.

Sheep Don't Go to School doesn't aim to be a representative anthology of Eastern European children's poetry. It is more a ragbag, a good read and a little coracle on the sea of imagination. I hope you enjoy it, whether you are six or sixty-six!

ANDREW FUSEK PETERS

Sheep Don't Go to School

Hear this most amazing feat,
Once they built a school for sheep!
Whoever did not speak, but bleat,
The greatest deal of praise would reap.

Whoever never went there
Was given a special prize
So no one went and the sheep school shut
Which comes as no surprise!

Sándor Weöres, 1913-89 *(Hungarian)*
[LV/AFP]

A Boy's Head

In it there is a space-ship
and a project
for doing away with piano lessons.

And there is
Noah's ark,
which shall be first.

And there is
an entirely new bird,
an entirely new hare,
an entirely new bumble-bee.

There is a river
that flows upwards.

There is a multiplication table.
There is anti-matter.
And it just cannot be trimmed.

I believe
that only what cannot be trimmed
is a head.

There is much promise
in the circumstance
that so many people have heads.

Miroslav Holub, 1923-98 *(Czech)*
[IM]

A Thoughtful Riddle

At first a forest,
Followed by a field,
Hedged by two swords,
Underneath two spheres,
Then two threads hanging
And at last,
A nightingale singing.

(Albanian riddle: answer on page 95)
(EV/AFP)

Greg the Greek

Greg the Greek
Crossed the creek
And in that creek he stuck a stick.
A quick, strict crawfish gripped the stick,
Stuck out his claw and
Tweaked the Greek

(Russian tongue-twister)
[CR/YD]

Chant for a Child Who Is Hurt
(to be said over and over while rubbing the the hurt spot)

Take the cow to the field
Fetch some hay for the cow
Squeeze milk from the cow
Bring the milk to your mum
Take bread from your mum
Give the bread to the chief
Take a coat from the chief
Send the coat to the king
Gain a cane from the king
Lead the cow with the cane
Take the cow to the field etc...

(Estonian)
[MBu/AFP]

15

Schoolmaster

The window gives onto the white trees.
The master looks out of it at the trees,
for a long time, he looks for a long time
out through the window at the trees,
breaking his chalk slowly in one hand.
And it's only the rules of long division.
And he's forgotten the rules of long division.
Imagine not remembering long division!
A mistake on the blackboard, a mistake.
We watch him with a different attention
needing no one to hint to us about it,
there's more than difference in this attention.
The schoolmaster's wife has gone away,
we do not know where she has gone to,
we do not know why she has gone,
what we know is his wife has gone away.

His clothes are neither new nor in the fashion;
wearing the suit which he always wears
and which is neither new nor in the fashion
the master goes downstairs to the cloakroom.
'What's the matter? Where is that ticket?
Perhaps I never picked up my ticket.
Where is the thing?' Rubbing his forehead.
'Oh, here is is. I'm getting old.
Don't argue auntie dear, I'm getting old.
You can't do much about getting old.'
We hear the door below creaking behind him.

The window gives onto the white trees.
The trees there are high and wonderful,
but they are not why we are looking out.
We look in silence at the schoolmaster.
He has a bent back and clumsy walk,
he moves without defences, clumsily,
worn out, I ought to have said, clumsily.
Snow falling on him softly through silence
turns him to white under the white trees.
He whitens into white like the trees.
A little longer will make him so white
we shall not see him in the whitened trees.

Yevgeny Yevtushenko *(Russian)*
[PL/RMG]

17

The Dancing Carrot

The beetroot was getting married,
The celery squealed with delight,
The carrot stood up to dance a jig
And the horseradish whistled all night.

(Czech)
[AFP]

The Door

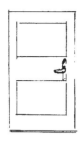

Go and open the door.
   Maybe outside there's
   a tree, or a wood,
   a garden,
   or a magic city.

Go and open the door.
  Maybe a dog's rummaging.
  Maybe you'll see a face,
or an eye,
or the picture
        of a picture.

Go and open the door.
  If there's a fog
  it will clear.

Go and open the door.
  Even if there's only
  the darkness ticking,
  even if there's only
  the hollow wind,
  even if
      nothing
          is there,
go and open the door.

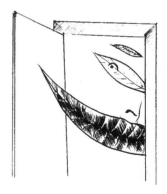

At least
there'll be
a draught.

Miroslav Holub *(Czech)*
[IM]

The Earth

The earth is round
one great ball,
kid in the playground
shoots for goal –
Ball flies high,
summer is nigh,
ball descends,
the summer ends.

Ottó Orbán *(Hungary)*
[GSz]

Walnut

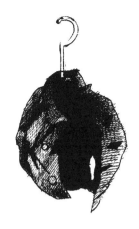

The pale green coat
of the walnut has split,
small wonder, since spring
he has been wearing it.

Autumn could mend it
with gossamer thread
but would stitches hold
for the winter ahead?

The wind gathers strength
over field and road
and shakes the walnut
out of his coat.

István Pákolitz, 1919-96 *(Hungary)*
[LV]

While the Leaves Were Still Green

While the leaves were still green,
We ate marmalade and bread,
But when the winter comes again,
Just walnuts and eggs painted yellow and red!

(traditional Yugoslavian)
[NB/AFP]

A Winter Dream

The bears in their den,
Bugs sleepy again,
Storm sings their song
All winter long,
Dreams in their head,
With snow for their bed.

Dora Gabe *(Bulgaria)*
[FB/AFP]

Winter

In the night,
Came a white horse to visit,
His hooves made no sound
As he covered the ground,
And snow filled the land with its spirit.

(Czech)
[AFP]

Riddle Me Night

In dark fields where
Grass never grew,
A grey horse grazes
All night through.

Nil Hilevič *(Bielarus riddle: answer on page 95)*
[VR]

Riddle Me Day

It rolls over rock, and never gets torn
It runs through the bush untouched by the thorn
It falls into water, but cannot sink down
It dives in the sea, yet cannot drown

(traditional Albanian riddle: answer on page 95)
[EV/AFP]

Winter Trees

Aren't you cold and won't you freeze,
With branches bare, you winter trees?
You've thrown away your summer shift,
Your autumn gold has come adrift.

Dearie me, you winter trees,
What strange behaviour if you please!
In summer, you could wear much less,
But come the winter, you undress!

Zoltán Zelk *(Hungary)*
[GSz]

25

Snow

A wonder came – I slept my fill;
At dawn the snow fell thick and still,
Early-early.

And over all the yard it lies,
Covering sheds and wood-supplies;
Purely-purely.

We have a tablecloth for best,
That glistens so to greet the guest,
Whitely-whitely.

The snow witched pettiness away,
Nor word nor shout nor laughter stay –
Quietly-quietly.

Silent, in quietude apart
I stand, with lightness in my heart,
Brightly, brightly.

Nil Hilevič *(Bielarus)*
[VR]

The Hare's House

Underneath a clump of broom
Hare has built himself a home.
What a builder, what a home,
All around the cold winds roam.

He blocked the windows up with moss,
Barred the door with cones across,
What a palace for a hare,
You'll see all the world from there!

From above, the house is hid
With some bracken for a lid!
What a cosy nook! You'll not
Without a fur coat sleep a jot!

And in winter, while you drowse,
Snowstorm sneaks into the house,
And Jack Frost will get in too,
They will freeze you till you're blue!

If he's not to freeze up quite,
Hare must jump about all night!
What a hare! And what a home,
Underneath the clump of broom!

Maksim Tank, 1912-95 *(Bielarus)*
[VR]

A Poem About Two Seals

The North Pole sweetshop tends to stay
Closed twenty-four hours a day,
Yet any time from nine till four
A sealboy and sealgirl are
Sure to be waiting at the door.
What seals find enticing
Is cake with lots of icing!
And should you want cocoa made of snow,
The little Polar corner shop
That never seems to open up
Is the only place to go.

Zoltán Zelk *(Hungary)*
[GSz]

I Had a Cricket

Once upon a time
I had a cricket,
He liked my song
And learned to sing it

Or was it I who
On a snowy day
Learned it from him
To while the cold away?

All winter long
In jolly full swing
He perched in my room
And continued to sing

Then we began
To chirrup together,
Our high spirits capered
In spite of the weather.

By the end of winter
I couldn't quite see
Who was the cricket,
Him or Me?

Erzsi Gazdag *(Hungary)*
[LV]

The Bear's Dilemma

Winter's going, here comes spring,
Grizzly bear sits pondering:
Back to sleep or time to wake?
What a terrible choice to make!

To leave the cave? Explore the wood?
There might be berries. Could be good.
And is the honey nice and sticky?
That is the question. Oh how tricky!

Sándor Weöres, 1913-89 *(Hungary)*
[GSz]

How a Pair of Spring Boots
Were Bought

A pair of blue,
Children's shoes,
Wished to choose
Their new mistress,
'Whose feet are fit for us?
She must be a nimble lass,
She cannot be a lazy ass!
With such a one,
We'll have such fun
And roam the seas!'
Sang the shoes,
Bright and blue,
Who found the girl,
And off they flew
around the world.

(Czech)
[AFP]

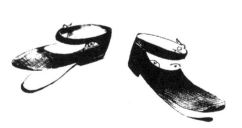

Summer Rain

Here it is so quiet
you can hear the twigs
whispering to each other.
Every leaf sags
under the heavy gold of the sun.
Such a wealth of gold
even the day stands still
holds its breath
to keep the gold from spilling
down into the weeds and underbrush.

Georgi Djagarov *(Bulgaria)*
[RH]

The Saddle of Gold

Two yellow stallions
Swam from the sea,
One with a saddle
Of golden leaves,
The other, a bridle
Of silken sheaves.
Which shall I ride?
And who shall it be?

Oh my heart would be bold
Though it never told
So I danced with the steed
In his silken fold,
Then I mounted the other
With his saddle of gold.
I shod him in silver
And fed him on hay:
Now fly to the mountains
For the break of the day!

(traditional Latvian)
[IH/AFP]

The Fairy Horse

A girl threw an apple to a cloud,
And the cloud kept the apple.
The girl prayed to all the clouds:
Brother clouds, give my back my golden apple.
The guests have arrived:
My mother's brothers and my uncles.
Their horses are wild like mountain fairies.
When they tread the dust
The dust doesn't rise.
When they tread on water,
Their hooves don't get wet.

(traditional Serbian)
[CS]

34

The Merry Dance

When Wolf did a dance with Billy-goat white
Bear played the pipes with his paws,
The Ram began to brew some beer
While Cat washed up and licked her claws!

(traditional Czech)
[AFP/VFP]

35

Where Have You Been?

Where have you been, billy-goat mine?
At the mill, at the mill, my little lord.

What were you doing there, billy-goat mine?
Milled and grinded, my little lord.

How did you measure it, billy-goat mine?
With my horn, with my horn, my little lord.

How did you sweep, billy-goat mine?
With my beard, with my beard, my little lord.

Did you eat there too, billy-goat mine?
Yes I did, yes I did, my little lord.

What did you eat there, billy-goat mine?
Baked turnip, white bread, my little lord.

Did you drink there too, billy-goat mine?
Yes I did, yes I did, my little lord.

What did you drink there, billy-goat mine?
Milk and honey, milk and honey, my little lord.

Did they flog you, billy-goat mine?
Yes they did, yes they did, my little lord.

How did they flog you, billy-goat mine?
With a rod on my ribs, my little lord.

Did you bleat then, billy-goat mine?
Yes I did, yes I did, my little lord.

How did you bleat then, billy-goat mine?
Bah! and *Bah!* my little lord.

(Latvian)
[AM/IH]

Storks

Stork so tall, long legged friend,
Where does the world begin and end?

You see the reeds there by the pond –
There's nothing of the world beyond.

Stork so tall with legs so thin,
Where then does the world begin?

Well stocked and fringed with fern and frond,
The pond is all. The world's the pond.

Zoltán Zelk *(Hungary)*
[GSz]

37

If Only

If only the deer grew feathered wings
It would be swift as a bird flying by;
And none of us would ever starve
If only bread would fall from the sky!

If only the ragdoll learned how to sow,
She'd be a seamstress stitching silk;
And we'd be stuffing our faces with cheese
If only the Sava flowed with milk!

If only it was always May,
Every stove would be out of a job;
And we'd all be gulping delicious fish-stew
If only the Danube were a boiling tub!

But since this is all imagination,
We might as well stop this conversation!

Jovan Jovanović Zmaj, *d.1904 (Serbian)*
[EDG/JL/AFP]

Animal Friends

Life is good
On the edge of the wood;
My stags take a bow,
Their horns to plough.
Six deer harrow,
Wolf digs a furrow;
Helped by fox
As strong as an ox.
With a stutter
Crow churns butter,
Lark from the stable
Sets the table.
Rabbit threshes,
Magpie brushes,
His tail like a broom,
Sweeping the room.

(traditional Latvian)
[IH/AFP]

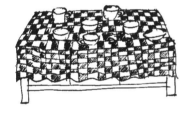

Playing Icarus

I went begging to the birds
And each of them gave me
A feather.

A high one from the vulture,
A red one from the bird of paradise,
A green one from the humming-bird,
A talking one from the parrot,
A shy one from the ostrich –
Oh, what wings I've made for myself.

I've attached them to my soul
And I've started to fly.
High flight of the vulture,
Red flight of the bird of paradise,
Green flight of the humming bird,
Talking flight of the parrot,
Shy flight of the ostrich –
Oh, how I've flown!

Marin Sorescu, 1936-96 *(Romania)*
[DJE/IRG]

Butterfly

Fly to me, fly butterfly,
I'll give you milk galore.
And if you drink, I'll give you more,
And if you drink, I'll give you more.

(Hungarian)
[LV]

A Competition

The cuckoo and the donkey
Had a row one day,
Which of them could sing the best
To greet the month of May.

The cuckoo says: 'It's me you ass!'
And starts out with his calls.
'Oh, I can do that better!'
The stupid donkey bawls.

Their song is sweet and lovely,
Fills everyone with awe,
For both of them are singing:
'Cuckoo, cuckoo, eeyore!'

Hoffmann von Fallersleben, 1798-1874 *(German)*
[TB]

43

To Say Aloud and Annoy
Anyone Who Will Listen!

A doggy stole a sausage,
From the big, bad butcher,
The butcher came and found her
And hit her with a hammer!
All the doggies cried,
They dug a little hole,
And on the doggy's gravestone,
They wrote this little tale:

A doggy stole a sausage,
From the big, bad butcher,
The butcher came and found her
And hit her with a hammer!
All the doggies cried,
They dug a little hole,
And on the doggy's gravestone,
They wrote this little tale:

A doggy stole a sausage,
From the big, bad butcher,
The butcher came and found her
And hit her with a hammer!
All the doggies cried,
They dug a little hole,
And on the doggy's gravestone,
They wrote this little tale...

(Czech)
[AFP]

A DOGG

Riddle Me This!

A white pigeon
Flew in,
Softly rustled
White wings
And in half an hour
Unfurled
News from the whole
Wide world.

Nil Hilevič *(Bielarus: answer on page 95)*
[VR]

Riddle Me That!

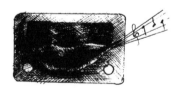

This is something quite small
With no tongue at all,
It can't drink or eat
A thing
But it speaks
And can sing.

Nil Hilevič *(Bielarus: answer on page 95)*
[VR]

Honza and the Princess

The princess with her golden curls
Lost her necklace strung with pearls.
Her father, the mightiest of mighty kings
Summoned Honza, the silliest of all the princelings:
'Honza! My daughter is in distress,
Find some pearls for my poor princess!'

Honza ran off with a spring in his toes,
To a farm where he bought a pound of potatoes,
He tipped them out in front of the king:
'Pearls for my princess I now bring,
Bigger and better than what you lost,
And these can be cooked for your breakfast!'

(Czech)
[AFP]

(In Czech tales, Honza is the fool who ends up outwitting everyone else)

The Cat and the Chef

A chef, who'd learned his ABC
And often held forth volubly,
Proposed that Puss should guard the grub
One day, and vanished to the pub
(He was a pious sort of man
And wished to toast his long-dead gran).
When he got back, he raised a cry.
The floor was strewn with scraps of pie,
And, almost hidden by a cask,
Greedily warming to his task,
His purr so loud it was a growl,
Puss Peter munched a whole roast fowl.

'O Glutton Cat! O Reprobate!'
Chef raged a while and then he tried
Reproaches more elaborate!
'Aren't you ashamed? Dear cat, reflect!
These four walls see your sinful luncheon.
People are talking. Where's your pride?
Have you no feline self-respect?'
Puss Peter listened and kept munching.

'Once, you were virtuous and refined,
To mice alone a cause of grief.
Now all the neighbours say *That thief!*
Pete's a poacher, Pete's a fiend,
We'd no more let a beast so hard
Set foot indoors – or in the yard –
Than we'd invite a wolf to sleep
Tucked in the pen among the sheep.
That little vandal, he wants punching.
He's a disease, an epidemic,
An oil-spill on the whole world's coast!'
There was no end to this polemic
But Peter Puss just went on munching
Till he'd demolished all the roast.

The moral's this: you brainy cooks
Who talk as if you'd swallowed books,
And spin great eloquence from small fact,
Don't waste your breath when you should act.

I.A.Krilov, 1769-1844 *(Russian)*
[CR/YD]

49

Mrs Mouse

Mrs Mouse made some porridge,
Nice and hot
In a small green pot.
In ran the children
Through the door,
Scattered like crumbs
All over the floor.
Every little mouse had the tiniest bowl,
Every little mouse gave a great big howl
Because the pot was empty
And now there was no more!

(Czech)
[AFP]

Not a Very Mice Poem

Tom Cat, speak to me,
Sitting on your stone:
I think I'll go to Riga
With some mice from home:

Meat for the gentlemen
Roasted very nice!
Fur for the ladies coats
Woven in a trice
And tails for the coachman's whips,
They'll pay a pretty price,
If I go to Riga
With my pretty pile of mice!

(traditional Latvian)
[IH/AFP]

The Milk-Tooth Mouse

Mishka-mishka,
Mousey mouse,
In a corner of the house,
Find the baby tooth I lost.
It's left a gap just where I bite –
Give me another, strong and white!

(Russian)
[MB]

My Mad Granny

One fine day,
Granny took a tray
To bake a little pie.
But where is the pie?
Taken by a doggy!
Where is the doggy?
He ran down the road!
Where is the road?
Hidden by the grass!
Where is the grass?
Eaten by the cow!
Where is the cow?
She had a little calf!
Where is the calf?
He ploughed a little field!
Where is the field?
Woven up in wheat!
Where is the wheat?
Taken by the granny
To make a little pie
For her little grandbabby!

(traditional Yugoslavian)
[NB/AFP]

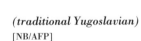

There Was a Little Boy

There was a little boy,
Who had some honey and bread.
There was a little girl,
Who ate it up instead!

(Czech)
[AFP]

If You Have a Worm
Inside Your Tummy

Put a small plate
On a big plate,
Place a pea on top as bait.
Put the plate
Under a crate
And wait.
If the worm comes out to eat,
That's great!
If not, it's not too late to
Put a small plate
On a big plate,
Place a pea on top as bait.
Put the plate
Under a crate
And wait.

If the worm comes out to eat,
That's great!
If not, it's not too late to
Put a small plate
On a big plate,
Place a pea on top as bait.
Put the plate
Under a crate
And wait.
If the worm comes out to eat,
That's great!
If not, it's not too late to...
(and on and on until all your friends are really BORED!)

(Czech)
[AFP/VFP]

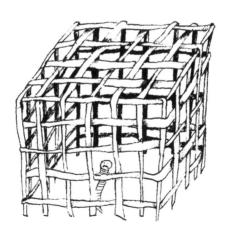

55

Thumb Boy

Long ago, all forlorn, a tiny boy was born,
Little Tom Nimble
Small as your thumb,
They bathed him in a thimble,
And rocked him in an egg shell,
Sleep Tom Thumb, sleep deep and well!

He stayed the size he was,
And never grew an inch,
He ate only poppy seeds,
One seed, two seeds, three at a pinch
And now he is quite full up,
But will he ever grow up?

And how does he play?
Tiny Tom-All-Alone in his house.
The dog barked 'I will eat you'.
The cat mistook him for a mouse,
Careful you might step on him,
Poor little Tom Slim!

His mother asked his grandmama,
'What shall give this little man?
To make him grow as if he were sprinkled
With a watering can?'
'If he works, he'll grow Tom Tall
There's jobs enough for all.'

56

Every day he works so hard,
He ends up with an empty tum,
Eats up all the bread and cake,
Every smidgen, morsel, crumb,
And now Tom Tum is smiling
For his mum is not so glum.

When he stops his work,
And has a moment spare,
He chases all the flies, and cries
'Touch the milk, if you dare
Shoo, Shoo, get away!
My mum wants fresh milk today!'

More and more, he grew and grew,
Out of his sleeves and tiny toys.
He no longer fits in an eggshell.
Now he's bigger than all the boys,
Tom Thumb, not so dumb,
Just might kick you up the bum!

(Czech)
[AFP]

The Ant Doctor

The Ant had broken her leg,
She bound herself up with a thread,
When the clock began to sing Midnight,
An Ant-Doctor ran to her bed.

The Doctor tapped on her heart,
And after, gave her this recipe:
Three times a day, a powder of sugar,
And soon you'll be better than best-can-be!

Miss Ant took the sugar-sweet powder,
Just as she had been told,
Each day she sat by the fire,
Each night she grew very cold.

She stayed in bed for four long days
On the fifth she started to cry:
Oh! Go away you bullying pain,
I do not want to die!

So then she blew on her broken leg,
And painted her toenails red!
Next morning, a happy and healthy Miss Ant,
Jumped right out of her bed!

(Czech)
[AFP]

Ant

The ant is carrying a crumb
Assisted by his dad and mum.
They're hurrying because the wind
Is dragging great rainclouds behind.

Were I the wind, I would waylay
The clouds and turn them all away
And scatter them across the sky
So that the ants could get home dry.

István Pákolitz, 1919-96 *(Hungary)*
[GSz]

Riddle Me Re

Not a horse, but has a saddle,
Not a ram, but has a horn,
Not a writer, but makes her mark;
What was the name with which she was born?

(Albanian riddle: answer on page 95)
[EV/AFP]

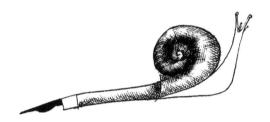

Dog & Cat

The dog has run down the lane,
The cat's crawled under the net,
And if it doesn't rain,
We won't get wet!

(Czech)
[AFP]

Three Hunters

Cat stalks mouse, dog has his eye
On cat, while in the sky,
An enormous thundercloud
Is stalking them both from on high.
Should it choose, it has the power,
To make both puss and puppy cower
Or send them scuttling through the shower.

Zoltán Zelk *(Hungary)*
[GSz]

Rain

Rain is falling, drops are dripping
the jester is full of complaint and gripe.
Meanwhile what does the old man do?
He lies on his stomach and smokes his pipe!

(traditional Hungarian)
[LV]

Short Verses About the Wind

1

Wind whips up a gust
Wind blows fit to bust,
Winter! thinks the bough
What does the wind want now?

2

Wind will huff and wind will blow,
Wind goes mumbling to and fro.
However snug it is within
The wind succeeds in getting in.

3

Roaring down the coastal shelf
The wind runs slap into itself,
Impossible to catch or check,
Its ankles high about its neck.

Sándor Weöres, 1913-89 *(Hungary)*
[GSz]

Fairy Tale

He built himself a house,
    his foundations
    his stones,
    his walls,
    his roof overhead,
    his chimney and smoke,
    his view from the window

He made himself a garden,
    his fence
    his thyme
    his earthworm
    his evening dew.

He cut out his bit of sky above.

And he wrapped the garden in the sky
And the house in the garden
and packed the lot in a handkerchief
and went off
lone as an Arctic fox
through the cold
unending
rain
into the world.

Miroslav Holub, 1923-98 *(Czech)*
[GT]

63

Praise Song of the Wind

Trees with weak roots
I will strike, I the wind.
I will roar, I will whistle.

Haycocks built today,
I will scatter, I the wind.
I will roar, I will whistle.

Badly made haycocks
I will carry off, I the wind.
I will roar, I will whistle.

Uncovered stacks of sheaves
I will soak through, I the wind.
I will roar, I will whistle.

Houses not tightly roofed
I will destroy, I the wind.
I will roar, I will whistle.

Hay piled in sheds
I will tear apart, I the wind.
I will roar, I will whistle.

Fire kindled in the road
I will set flickering, I the wind.
I will roar, I will whistle.

Houses with bad smoke holes,
I will shake, I the wind.
I will roar, I will whistle.

The farmer who does not think
I will make to think, I the wind.
I will roar, I will whistle.

The worthless slug-a-bed
I will wake, I the wind.
I will roar, I will whistle.

(traditional Siberian)
[WR/WRT]

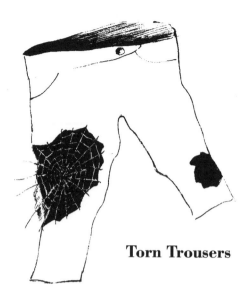

Torn Trousers

Trousers torn,
Wind blows in.
How to mend?
Spider Spin!

(Czech)
[AFP/VFP]

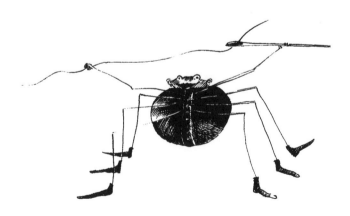

66

A Tale

Peace sleeps quiet
in a mountain cave.
She is still
but a bonny babe.
A gentle deer
comes to feed her,
and the web of a spider,
is woven to hide her.

Miklós Radnóti, 1909-44 *(Hungarian)*
[LV/AFP]

Such Times

I walk across the playground. And all of a sudden
a six-year-old boy rushes to me
with wild strawberry cheeks.
In his hand he clutches a pop gun.
'Bang! Bang!' – he shoots at me.
Then he sticks the weapon in his pocket.
'Gotcha!' – he says and runs off.

I notify the family. Friends.
I phone the police and report my death.
They spread their helpless hands.
'Such times' – they say.

Ewa Lipska *(Poland)*
[BP/TH]

A Walk

Not to get in the way at home,
I went out for a walk
And stuck myself like a stamp
To a bench in the middle of the park.
Then some pensioners came along
And said to me: 'Move over!'
So, not to get in the way of the old,
I once again walked in the park

Dragan Lukić *(Serbian)*
[EDG/JL]

For a Little Love

For a little love, I would go to the end of the world;
I would go with my head bare and feet unshod,
I would go through ice, but in my soul forever May,
I would go through the storm, but still hear the blackbird sing,
I would go through the desert, and have pearls of dew in my heart.
For a little love, I would go to the end of the world,
Like the one, who sings at the door and begs.

(FROM *Windows in a Storm*)
Jaroslav Vrchlický *(Czech)*
[VFP/AFP]

With Every Poem

With every poem, I become poorer
And richer for having given.
An unknown voice sings my poem;
I only pass on his words.

Tibor Tollas, 1920-97 *(Hungary)*
[LV]

Hunt

I never have been in pursuit of words.
All I ever looked for
Was traces of their passage
Like the long silver haul
Of sunlight sweeping the grass
Or moonblinds drawn on the sea.

The shadows of words
Are what I hunted –
And hunting these is a skill
Best learned from the elders.
The elders know
That nothing is more precious
In a word
Than the shadow it casts
And words with no shadows to cast
Have lost their word-souls.

Ana Blandiana *(Romania)*
[SH/SD/HB]

Ceremony

My poems boil
in cauldrons, in pots, in percolators.
The whole house smells of poetry
just like autumn,
as if my soul
were jam,
sticky, shiny, slimy
– a muddy memory of a plum.

Nina Cassian *(Romania)*
[AD/BW]

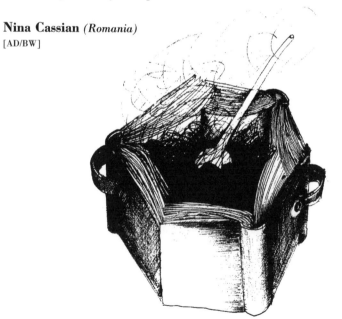

For My Poems

For my poems, written down so soon in life, so early,
I did not know I was a poet yet,
Forced loose from me like droplets from a fountain,
A rocket's sparking jet,

Poems storming from me, invading, like some tiny demons
The sanctuary where sleep and incense twine,
Their themes made up of youth and death, my poems,
My always unread lines!

Thrown here and there amid the dust of various bookshops,
Untouched then, now, by any reader's thumb,
For my poems, stored deep like wines of precious vintage,
I know a time will come.

Marina Tsvetayeva, 1892-1941 *(Russian)*
[DMcD]

Nothing

Blessed is the girl with nothing at all,
Never a worry where to hide it all;
Sleeps so lightly
Wakes up sprightly,
Nothing to steal, not a bean, nor a ball!

(Czech)
[AFP/VFP]

Lady Lack-Luck

I don't know where I'm going,
Hither or thence,
So I lock myself in,
And sit on the fence.
Turn the key on locks one, two and three,
Oh who will come and unlock me?
Quick! Lick a stamp, if you like,
Send a letter if you dare,
With a lock of lucky hair.
Then shall I be your wedded wife,
For the rest of our tick-tock life.
But for now, I don't know where I'm going,
Toing or froing,
Hither or thence,
So I lock myself in,
And sit on the fence.

(Czech)
[AFP]

Riddle Me These

Twelve geese
And sixty gosling
Two shepherds standing dozing!

(Albanian riddle: answer on page 95)
[EV]

There stands an oak
And from that oak,
Twelve branches grew,
And on each branch,
Nests two plus two
And in each nest,
Seven eggs bright blue.

(Czech riddle: answer on page 95)
[AFP]

Old Age

The hazel grove has put on purple satin,
a lime tree wears a gown of silky green.
But I shall not change again,
no one will look at me.

There are strange men
who make bundles of nettles and weeds
but where are the ones
who would kiss an old woman's hair?

I am alone.
Grandmother, they call me –
I feel like a dark spot
on the bright-hued rug of the world.

Maria Pawlikowska-Jasnorzewska, 1893-1945 *(Poland)*
[SB/PK]

There Is No Old Age

There is no old age! Only fruit and a flower,
and new wheat, and a seed and everything starts afresh,
Because the same angel, either in frost or early spring
spreads his youthful wings, and grows and grows and grows!

Kazimiera Iłłakowiczówna, 1892-1983 *(Poland)*
[SB/PK]

74

Angels

I saw one he came in a taxi the front seat
Was laid flat that way he had room
They lifted him out in front of the little fishmonger's
Escorted him into a shorn garden
There he stood serious in the air overtowered
Those who supported him nothing reached his eyes
His clothes were faded remnants of gold
Coated his chest he was without wings
His guides leaned him against a cart
Blocked the wheels before so he
Wouldn't begin to slide get smashed
I saw his hands they were empty
Probably carried the olive branch before or
Played a lyre for centuries
Now he was on his way in a taxi looking for an apartment
First to the antique shop what will become of him who
Really needs an angel who's that big
He fills a kitchen would stand
Where a refrigerator would make more sense or the table
With the bread-slicing machine, the solution
For him would be a kindergarten if it gave him shelter
Who wouldn't like to grow up with an angel

Sarah Kirsch *(Germany)*
[ML]

75

Carol

In the stable very sleepy
is a baby with no daddy.
The ox listens to his mummy
who's complaining to her baby,
that she gave birth in Bethlehem,
with no linen to swaddle him,
with no bands, with no water,
or rush light, or Godmother.
Joseph hung the circle from his hair
on a nail and left it there
and left, left for who knows where,
to be barked at by dogs everywhere.
Night is black, the hours pass slowly,
but mummy stays beside her baby.
And so that they will not be lonely,
an angel comes for company
and in the night deliberately
lights his finger brightly.
And now God's tall angel
burns like a tallow candle.

Lucian Blaga, 1895-1961 *(Romania)*
[BW/SA]

Song

There's a bird that comes flying
Settles down on my knee,
In his bill there's a letter
From my mother to me.

Little bird take the greeting,
Take a kiss and a tear,
For I cannot go with you
As I have to stay here.

(traditional German folksong)
[GM]

Fragment

My father lifted
a mouthorgan up
to the wind on a hill

and the wind of Bohemia
sighed a few
frail and blue notes

man and child
in a harebell light
frail ghosts... faint tune

Gerda Mayer *(from Karlsbad)*
[ENGLISH POEM]

Brotherless Sisters

Two sisters who had no brother
Made one of silk to share,
Of white silk and of red.
For his waist they used barberry wood,
Black eyes, two precious stones.
For eyebrows, sea leeches,
Tiny teeth a string of pearls.
They fed him sugar and honey sweet
And told him: now eat and then speak.

(traditional Serbian)
[CS]

The Bridge

Up to his knees in stream and spate
the bridge takes time to contemplate
the wheels that rumble down the track
over the water across his back,
and waves below where bright of fin
the fishes jostle round his shin.

Like a heron with wings of steel
he guards his watery commonweal.
Of little consequence to him
that as day passes, he grows slim:
on his faint limbs as it grows late,
dreams of both banks congregate.

Ernő Hárs *(Hungary)*
[GSz]

79

The Song of Doruntina

This traditional story-poem is well known to young people throughout Albania. The family has nine sons and one daughter who, against her mother's wishes, is married far away from her family. Konstandin, the youngest son, tries to make it up to his mother by promising to bring his sister, Doruntina, back on the Easter day, three years after she was married. But during that time, all the sons go off to war and are killed. Nevertheless, Konstandin keeps his promise from beyond the grave...

It was the Easter noon,
And mother in a swoon;
She broke at last her fast
And mourned for those she lost:
'Lord of the sun,
And Lord of the moon,
You killed each son
Too soon, too soon!
Bridges were burned
Cradles turned,
Dowries spurned,
How I yearned
For my fine sons,
Nine sons killed
In a hail of guns.'

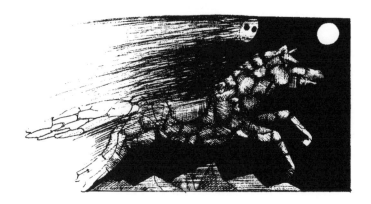

'Konstandin!
See the pain I am in!
The promise you made
In a coffin now laid...'

Konstandin, young brother
Lying in his grave,
Heard his mother.
He would be brave:
He climbed from the coffin,
Made a horse out of stone,
A saddle of mud,
And a bridle of bone.
He galloped so fast
To the sister they'd lost
As up in the sky,
The moon rode high.

At the house of his sister
The brother jumped down
With a deathly frown
And knocked on the midnight door.
'Welcome in,
My Konstandin,
You look so pale,
You seem so thin!
Has someone died?'
'Do not worry,' he lied
'Now come, we shall ride!'
And then they jumped
On his steed of stone,
And off they flew
Galloping home.

At the church he slowed,
He whispered 'Sister!'
His cold lips kissed her:
'I am the brother
Who promised our mother!
Now follow the road!'
And he turned
With his steed
To his graveyard abode.

Doruntina ran on
With a quickening pace.
Soon she would see
Her dear mother's face.
Up in the sky,
The moon rode high
As she knocked at the midnight door.
'Who is it for?'
said a voice from afar.
'Mother it is me,
your daughter fair!'

Her mother said,
'My sons are dead
And she is so far away!'
'Oh mother it is me
The promise was kept!'
'But my son is dead!'
The mother now wept,
'Dead in the ground
For three whole years!'
At that, her eyes
Filled up with tears.
'My dead son
Brought you here!'
'My dead brother
Held me near!'
The mother shook,
The daughter groaned,
The trees shivered,
The branches moaned,
Such love made fact!
Their bodies cracked
And shattered like glass
And crumbled to grass,
A promise kept three years too long,
This is the end of Doruntina's song.

(traditional Albanian)
[EV/AFP]

An Incredible Story

There was a little house
And in the little house,
There stood a little desk.
And on the little desk,
There sat a little saucer,
And in the little saucer
There was a little water,
And in the little water
There swam a little fish.

Oh! Where is the little fish?
The little cat has eaten her
For his little dish!
Oh! Where is the little cat?
In the little forest.
Oh! Where is the little forest?
Burned to a little dust.
Oh! Where is the little dust?
Blown to a little lake.
Oh! Where is the little lake?
Drunk by a little duck.
Oh! Where is the little duck?
Eaten by the little men.
Oh! Where are the men so brave?
DEAD AND BURIED IN A LITTLE GRAVE!

(Czech)
[AFP]

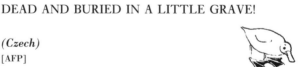

84

A Fussy Riddle

One day, it swept in through the door,
Rushed and fussed around the floor
Then jumped inside our wooden chest!
What can it be? Just one clue more:
It grew up in a forest...

(Czech: answer on page 95)
[AFP]

I Shall Tell a Silly Tale

I shall tell a silly tale:
The dog jumped over the milking pail.

A second tale now I shall tell:
The water poured from the weeping well.

The third that I shall tell to you:
The children slept in the chimney flue,

And when they had slept a long, long time,
They were fed with bread and told this rhyme!

(Czech)
[AFP]

The Spring

Spring went off to school
grew into a stream
feet pattering over stones
as if in a dream.

Having reached the fields
it widened into flood
grew thicker in the waist
green-brown with the mud.

Once through with the world
it grew to adulthood.
In the grey Councils of the Sea,
it sits now, for good.

Ottó Orbán *(Hungary)*
[GSz]

Evensong

Evening comes on, dusk grows cold,
Bunny ears must droop and fold.
Pussy purrs, curls up and sighs
Mari darling close your eyes.

(Hungarian)
[GSz]

Albanian Proverbs

1. Each hand washes the other,
   Both wash the face.

2. Love your homeland
   As the eagle its nest.

3. The tongue has no bones,
   But it breaks bones.

[EV]

Mother Scarlet

There she goes, there she goes
Mother Scarlet's daughter,
Scarlet clad, velvet clad,
Wreaths of pearls about her head.
I must go, my bridges burn,
Nevermore will I return
Scarlet clad, velvet clad
Wreath of pearls about my head.

(Hungarian)
[GSz]

Before Going to Sleep: 1

Tell me…
Is it easy to make thunder?
And when will the birds' nests be ripe?
How does the wind whistle his song?
And where does raven sleep at night?
And above all, that rain I'm seeing,
Up in Heaven, are they weeing?!

František Halas *(Czech)*
[VFP/AFP]

Stars

While walking home with my tiny son
Summer dusk falling into evening blue,
Chirping of crickets laced the silence
And in the dark sky, a star forest grew.

My son stopped and was full of wonder
For he had never seen so many stars,
He thought them crickets with eyes of fire
And they filled the heavens from moon to Mars.

Then he gave me news of the marvel,
The sky above aglow with light:
Do you hear, father? How beautiful,
All the stars are singing tonight.

Tibor Tollas, 1920-97 *(Hungary)*
[LV]

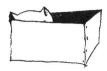 

Bird

Alack, alack, alack,
it's time to hit the sack.
The eyelid bird grows heavy,
the sky is turning black.

The bird is singing weep, weep weep,
time for Kate to go to sleep.
Look how mummy's eyes are closing
She herself is gently dozing.
Pussycat has long forgot
to purr inside her shoebox cot,
she's snoring somewhere in her head.
The little bird grows wings of lead,
into the sack, I saw you yawn!
Off with you now – Go fly till dawn.

Ottó Orbán *(Hungary)*
[GSz]

Fall Asleep My Beauty Boy

Fall asleep my beauty boy
And dream a tattle tale,
Of knights who brave the fairy sky
With eyes of moony pale.

They ride the bare-black fields of night
With horses dapple grey,
Cradling their curving swords,
Each blade a golden ray.

The birds are filled with fairy fear
At the hoofbeats stamping by,
Their song is filled with dread and drear
As they fly to the feathered sky.

Oh fairy birds, fair fairy birds!
Be quiet a little while,
And let the dream of my beauty boy
Be soft as a slumbering smile.

And you, brave knights, with eyes of cold,
Now hush your clattering swords,
My son still needs his beauty sleep
So whisper your warrior words.

Oh my brave knights, the night is long
Please let my beauty be,
And leave the land of darkened dream
And fly to the fairy-tale sea.

Jozef Czechowicz *(Poland)*
[LG/AFP]

Before Going to Sleep: 2

It might sound silly, Dad,
But I tell you it's true,
There's a bird on the lawn,
Tying up his shoe!
His shoelace wriggled,
Then unwrapped,
The blackbird tugged,
The shoelace snapped!
With a smile on his face,
He ate up the lace!
How can he get one, how oh how?
Where can buy a new one now?

Said Dad,
'What did they teach you
At school this term?
Just wait for the dawn and you'll see,
IT'S A WORM!

Frantisek Halas *(Czech)*
[VFP/AFP]

Hovercraft

On the quiet midnight hour,
Pyjamas and hovercraft fill the sky,
In village and city they take off from beds,
One then another, it's time to fly.

Some are small as a fluffed-up pillow,
Others as big as a king-sized bed,
Without the slightest need of gas,
Their engines are on feathers fed.

No sooner is the light switched off,
Pyjama passengers sigh *Goodnight!*
The hovercraft rises silent and soft,
The tour has begun, now hold on tight!

The journey ends with the hovering of dawn
Out of the night and into the day,
They make a perfect bedroom landing,
Leave their passengers and fly away.

If you are lucky, at the edge of the bed,
You might just find a tiny feather
The hovercraft dropped on its return
In a dream of stormy weather.

Wanda Chotomska *(Poland)*
[LG/AFP]

ANSWERS TO RIDDLES

ACKNOWLEDGEMENTS

Acknowledgements are due to these publishers for their kind permission to reprint poems by these authors from their books: **Anvil Press Poetry Ltd,** for Sarah Kirsch from *Winter Music,* trs. Margitt Lehbert (1994); **Bloodaxe Books Ltd,** for Ana Blandiana from *When the Tunnels Meet: Contemporary Romanian Poetry,* ed. John Fairleigh (1997), Miroslav Holub from *Poems Before & After: Collected English Translations* (1990), Marin Sorescu from *The Biggest Egg in the World* (1987), Marina Tsvetayeva from *Selected Poems,* trs. David McDuff (1987); **Forest Books,** for Nina Cassian from *Call Me Alive,* trs. Andrea Deletant & Brenda Walker (1994), Georgi Djagarov, trs. Richard Harteis from *Poets of Bulgaria,* ed. William Meredith (1990), Kazimiera Illakowiczówna and Maria Pawlikowska-Jasnorzewska from *Ariadne's Thread: Polish Women Poets,* trs. Susan Bassnett & Piotr Kuhiwczak (1988), and Ewa Lipska from *Poet? Criminal? Madman?* trs. Barbara Plebanek & Tony Howard (1991); **Penguin Books Ltd,** for Yevgeny Yevtushenko from *Selected Poems* (1962).

Copyright to these translations is controlled by the above publishers, and to the other translations first published in this book to the translators listed on page 8. Thanks are also due to Charles Simic, for permission to reprint two of his translations from his book *The Horse Has Six Legs: An Anthology of Serbian Poetry* (Graywolf Press, 1992); to Gerda Mayer, for 'Fragment', first published in *Ariel* and reprinted from *Bernini's Cat* (Iron Press, 1999); to Brenda Walker for 'Carol', from Lucian Blaga's *Complete Poems* (1999); and to Carol Rumens and Yuri Drobyshev for translations first published in *The Honest Ulsterman.*

Every effort has been made to trace copyright holders of the translations included in this book. The editor and publisher apologise if any material has been included without permission or without the appropriate acknowledgement, and would be glad to be told of anyone who has not been consulted.